YOU AND YOUR BODY

Your Brain and Nervous System

Dorothy Baldwin and Claire Lister

The Bookwright Press
New York · 1984

YOU AND YOUR BODY

Some words in these books are
printed in **bold**, and their meanings
are explained in the glossary on
page 30.

First published in the United States in 1984 by
The Bookwright Press, 387 Park Avenue South, New York, NY 10016

First published in 1983 by Wayland (Publishers) Limited
49 Lansdowne Place, Hove, East Sussex BN3 1HF, England
©Copyright 1983 Wayland (Publishers) Limited

ISBN 0-531-04800-4

Library of Congress Catalog Card Number 83-72786

Series designed by Behram Kapadia
Illustrated by Nicholas Cannan

Printed in Italy by G. Canale & C. S.p.A. Turin

Contents

Chapter 1

Your Brain and Nerves

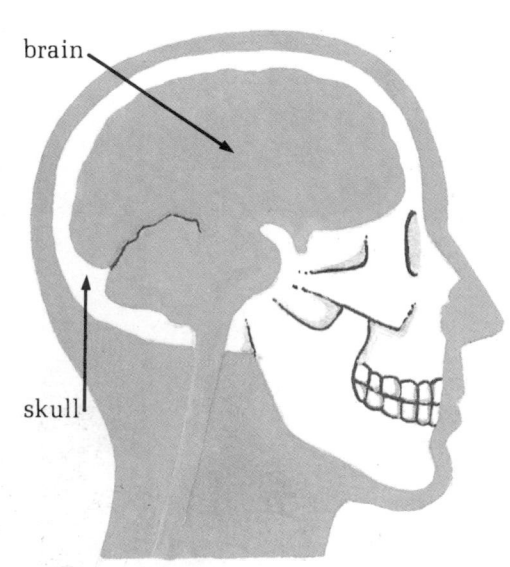

brain

skull

Put your hands to your head and feel your skull. Start at your eyebrows, go up your forehead, then spread your fingers wide over the huge circle of bone. Inside all that space is your brain. You can see from the diagram how big it is.

What does your brain look like?

Some people say it looks like a large wrinkled walnut. It is made up of thousands of millions of nerve cells, and is quite heavy. The brain of an average adult weighs about 1.5kg (3.3lb) — compare that with a package of sugar!

Your brain is still growing. Eating **protein** foods is important for brain growth. From the chart, can you work out when the brain grows fastest?

Brain cells are delicate — your hard skull doesn't actually touch your brain. There are three linings between them. They are called the **meninges**. The outer lining is a tough protection against your bony skull. The two inside linings are delicate — like lacy cobwebs. The space between them is filled with a special fluid and a great many tiny blood tubes called **capillaries**.

Weight of brain in relation to age

age in years	weight of brain
newborn	382g (13oz)
1	908g (32oz)
2	993g (35oz)
3	1124g (39oz)
4	1234g (43oz)
5	1242g (43.5oz)
6	1312g (45.9oz)
7	1322g (46.2oz)
10	1344g (47oz)

Feeding your brain

Whether you are awake, asleep, thinking hard or just day dreaming, your brain must have lots of oxygen all the time. In fact, after five minutes without oxygen, brain cells die. This is serious because brain cells are different from other cells. They cannot mend themselves if they are damaged, and they cannot be replaced once they are dead.

To keep your brain well-fed with oxygen, your heart pumps a great deal of blood into it. The blood flows into the capillaries lining your brain so that the special fluid between the meninges becomes rich in dissolved oxygen and food.

This model shows the network of blood tubes that feed the brain.

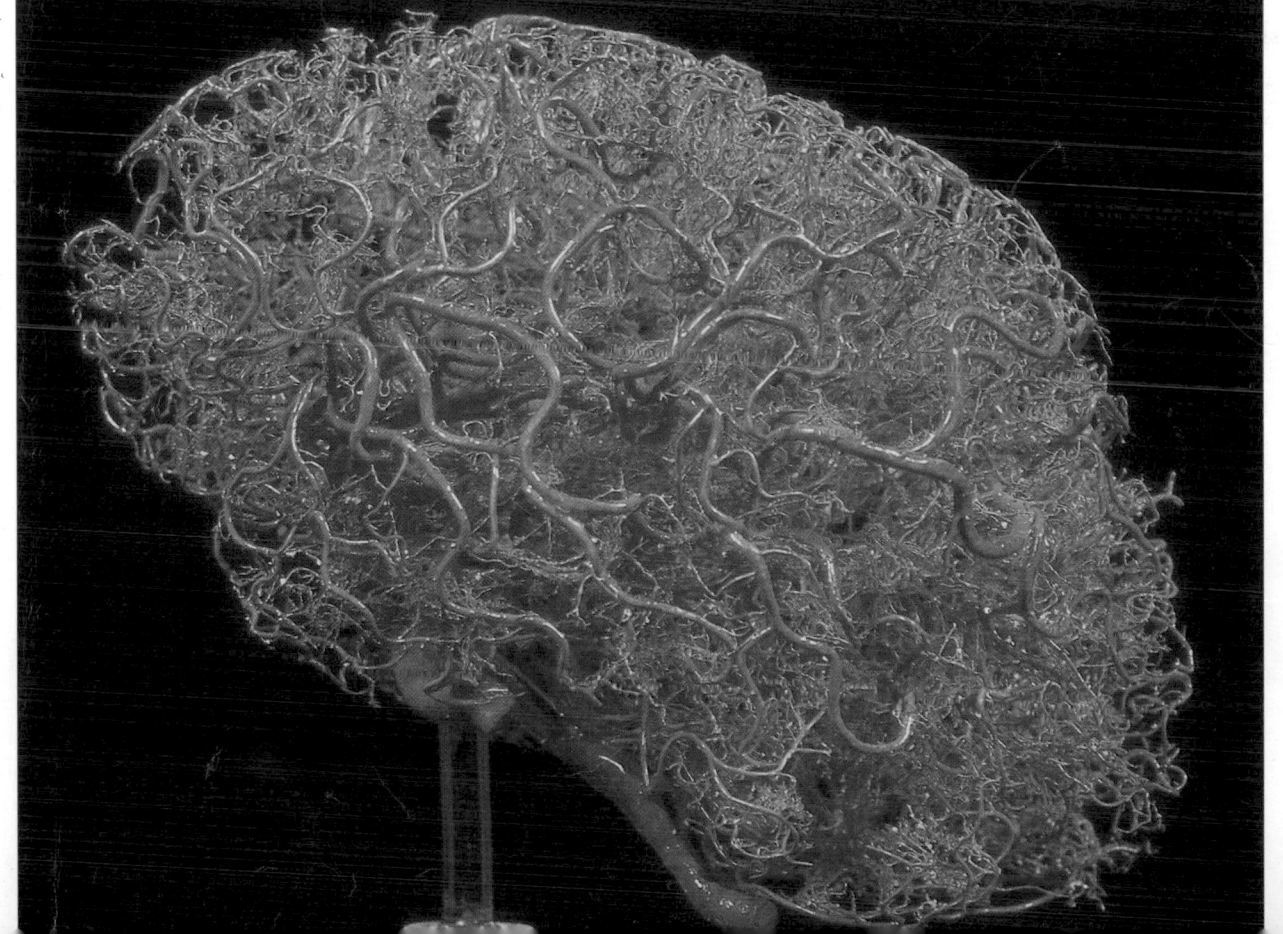

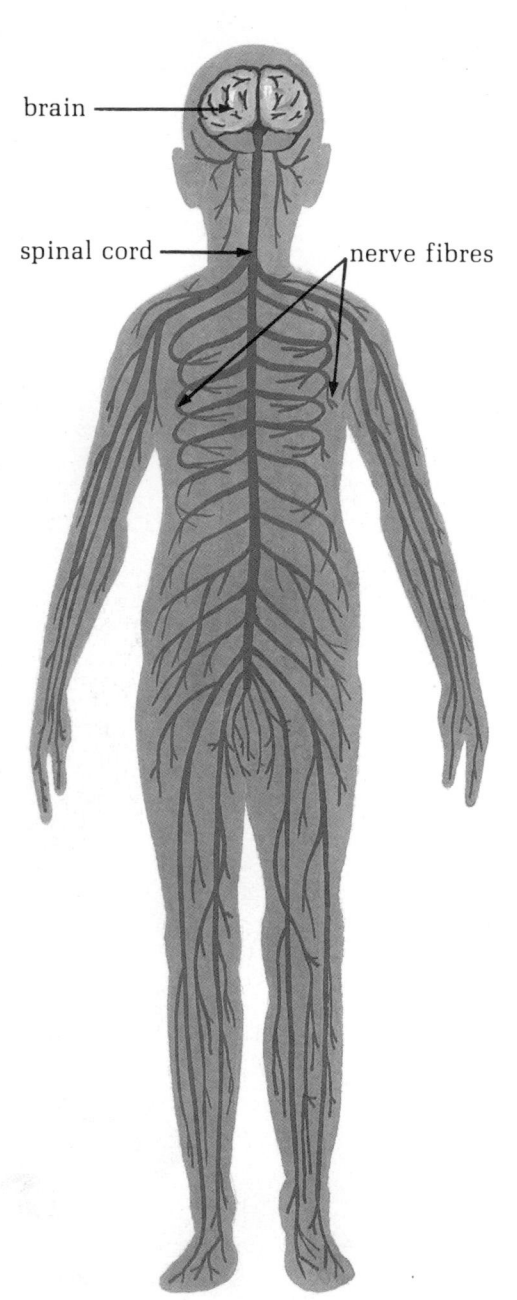

brain

spinal cord

nerve fibres

If enough blood is not pumped up to your brain, you faint. Once you have fallen down, the blood can easily flow to your brain, and you come around again. But fainting feels unpleasant, and you could hit your head when you fall. Make sure you put your head down between your knees the moment you begin to feel faint.

Your spinal cord and nerves

Your brain doesn't stop at the back of your skull. It goes on, down your **spinal cord**. Your spinal cord is made of **nerve fibers** and nerve cells. The fibers are for passing messages to and from your brain. These messages are called **nerve impulses**. They are like traveling waves of electrical and chemical changes. They can travel at terrific speed — along a large nerve fiber an impulse can travel at 200 miles an hour!

Your spinal cord is bathed in the same fluid as the brain, and it is protected by the knobbly bones of your spine.

In the diagram notice how the nerve fibers spread out from the brain and spinal cord. They go to all parts of your body. Their work is communication. Some nerve fibers carry information to your brain. Others bring back instructions from your brain, telling your muscles what to do. Some nerve fibers only carry messages to and from your spinal cord. Very simple messages can be dealt with by the nerve cells of the spinal cord. All other impulses must be interpreted (made sense of) and then dealt with, by your brain. The pictures on this page show how this works.

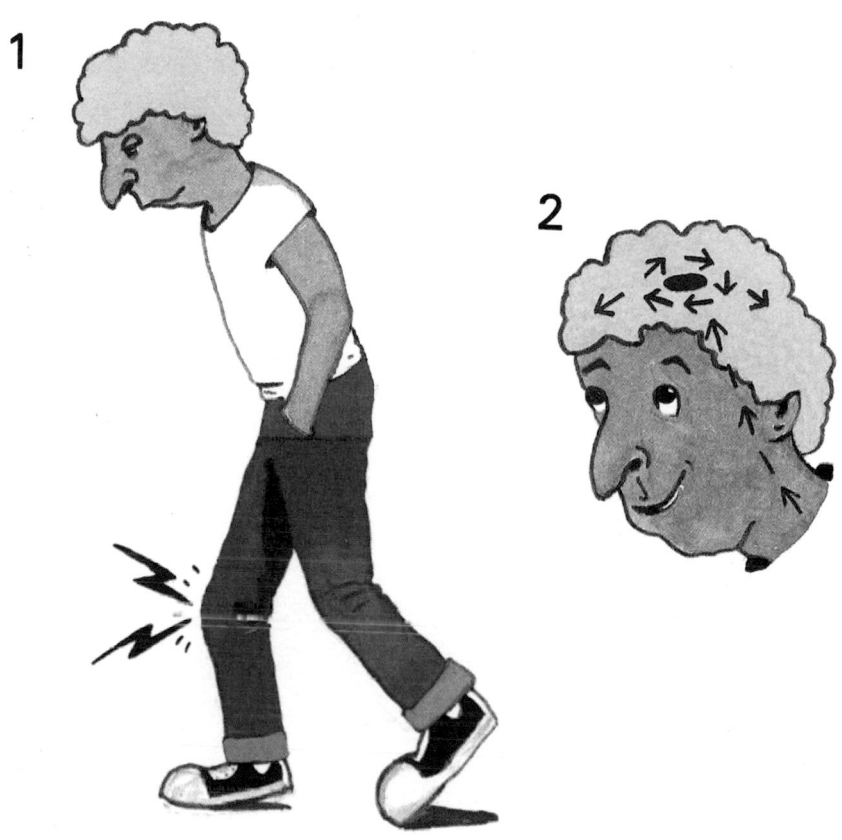

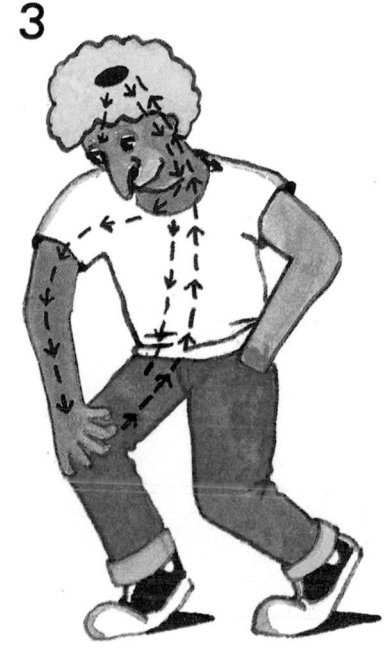

1 Your knee itches. The itchy sensation is picked up and sent flashing along nerve fibers to your brain.

2 Your brain interprets what the impulses mean. It then decides what to do about the itch. It passes new information to other parts of your brain.

3 New impulses are flashed out from your brain. Notice that the information goes to more than one place. The muscles of your eyes, fingers, arms, back and legs are all given instructions to help you scratch.

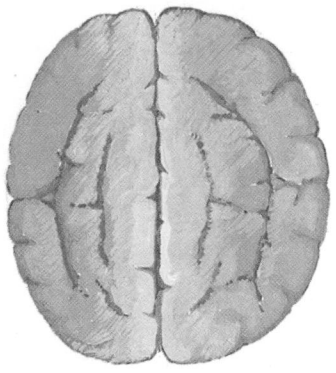

Above *This view of the top of the brain shows how the cerebrum is divided in half.*

Below *The cerebrum deals with the decisions you make when you play a game.*

The parts of your brain

The biggest part of your brain is the **cerebrum**. It is divided into two halves. The left half of the cerebrum controls the right side of your body, and the right half controls the left side of your body. This fact was discovered when it was noticed that people who had **strokes** couldn't move their right hand although it was the left side of their brain that was damaged.

The cerebrum controls your conscious actions — the movements under the control of your will. However, it also deals with other things which are not completely understood. These are interesting sides of people — thinking, decision-making, memory, emotions and imagination.

Tucked under the large cerebrum is the **cerebellum**. This word means "little brain." The cerebellum receives messages from your **semicircular canals** in your ears, and the **stretch receptors** in your muscles. It controls your balance and movement by putting together all the messages and then sending out new ones so that your actions will be smooth and coordinated.

At the top of your spinal cord is the **medulla**. This deals with your **involuntary muscles** which are involved in breathing, heartbeat and digestion. The medulla works at an unconscious level because it must work even while the conscious part of your brain is asleep. You wouldn't be alive now if your medulla could fall asleep!

The cerebellum controls your sense of balance and coordination.

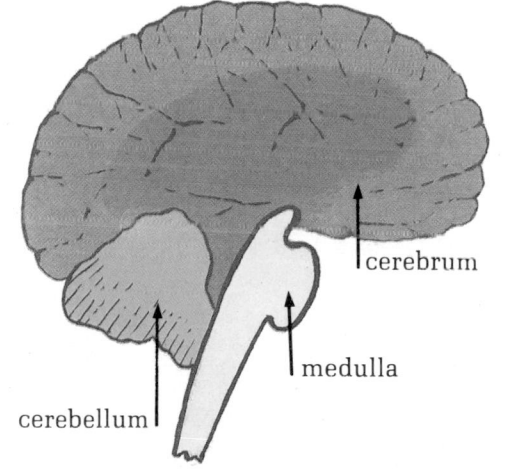

cerebrum

medulla

cerebellum

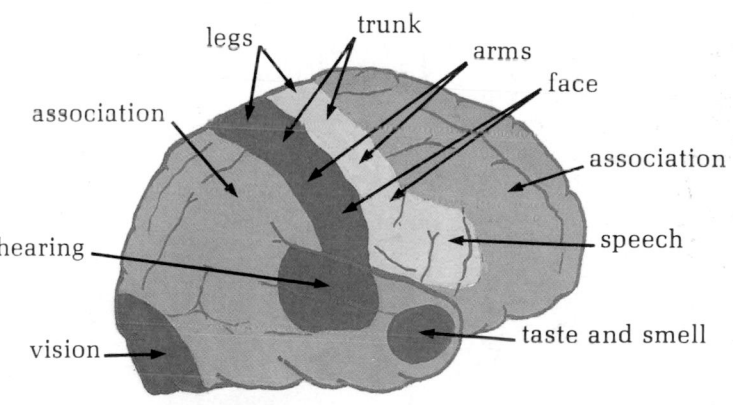

legs

trunk

arms

face

association

association

hearing

speech

vision

taste and smell

■ Information coming in.

■ Information being dealt with.

□ Information going out.

Chapter 2

Actions and Reactions

This is how to cross your legs to test the reflex action in your knee.

Your reflex actions

Sit exactly like the person in the picture. Your knee should be resting so that your upper leg hangs loose. With the edge of your palm, give a sharp blow to the place just below your kneecap. If you do this correctly, your leg will suddenly shoot out. Did you have to think about moving your leg? Try it again. Notice how your leg shoots out without any control from you. This is a **reflex action** — an automatic action you are born with and do not control. Can you think of any others?

While you were testing your knee reflex, did you notice your swallowing reflex? Or your blinking reflex?

Some reflexes, such as blinking or breathing, can be controlled by your will. But you can only do it for a short time. Nobody can hold their breath, or not blink, after a while. A reflex action is very powerful — it helps to keep you alive.

Conditioned reflexes

Imagine you are sucking a bitter lemon. Can you feel extra **saliva** running into your mouth? If you imagine sucking the end of a pencil, nothing happens. Why?

In 1902, a famous Russian scientist called Pavlov also wondered why. He had noticed how saliva dripped from the mouth of a dog when it saw its bowl of food. But a puppy isn't born knowing what a bowl of food looks like, so what had the dog learned that made the saliva come automatically? Pavlov thought up the experiment shown in these pictures:

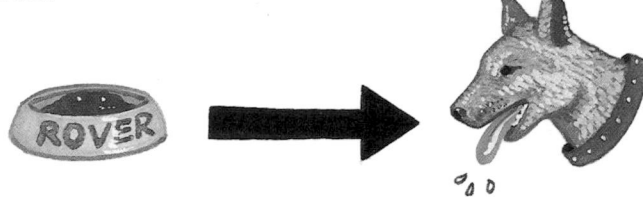

1 *The dog's saliva always flows when he sees his bowl of food.*

2 *A bell is rung every time the dog is given his bowl of food.*

3 *The dog has learned to associate the bell with food, and his saliva flows when he hears the bell ring, even if there is no food.*

The result shows the same reaction as that extra saliva which comes when you think of eating a lemon. You have a "learned" or "conditioned" reflex because you know what to expect.

12   This actor is learning his lines by repeating them out loud.

Learning and memory

Pavlov had to do his experiment many times before the dog made the link or association between food and the bell. Other sorts of learning work in rather the same way. If you want to learn a poem, you have to repeat it over and over again. You have to pay attention to the words, and practice saying them out loud. At school you may have been told to pay attention, and thought that this is just something all teachers say. But it is much more than that — it is the secret of all real learning. You must concentrate with every bit of your energy, otherwise the information will not go into your brain. This boy thinks he is studying very hard, but he cannot be. There are too many distractions. His memory cannot really function.

It is difficult for this boy to concentrate on his book with so many distractions around him.

The "fight or flight" system

This is a very important part of your nervous system. Its correct name is the **autonomic system**. Autonomic comes from a Greek word meaning 'self government.' The autonomic system controls the actions you do without thinking — actions such as sweating and shivering. It also controls your body's reactions to the way you feel — hence its usual name "fight or flight."

For some people, the words "the teacher wants to see you," are enough to start up butterflies in the stomach. Are you one of these people? If so, you will know the dreaded symptoms. Your heart thumps

Does your "fight or flight" system start to work when you sit waiting to see the dentist?

loudly, your breathing rate increases and you go pale. You may feel sick, or start sweating — can you add any more?

These feelings are a perfectly natural reaction to fear. Fear can be real or imagined. Nowadays it is called feeling threatened. The minute you feel threatened, your body switches to instant defense. This is Nature's Law — you are protecting yourself against danger. The fight or flight system switches you to "action stations."

How the fight or flight system works

As your nervous system springs into action, it sends messages to the glands on top of your kidneys. They make a special **hormone** called **adrenaline,** (see page 26), which pours into your blood. Your heart starts to beat faster pumping the adrenaline throughout your body. You can see the results in the diagram.

You can understand now why you feel as if you have butterflies in your stomach, and other unusual feelings. Suddenly, your body has only one interest — to get you out of danger. It stops working on anything else.

So what happens next? Whether you stand your ground and fight, or take to your heels in flight, depends on the situation, and the sort of person you are. Often, you can't do either. You know you must accept whatever trouble you are in!

The fight or flight system was very important in bygone days when wild beasts

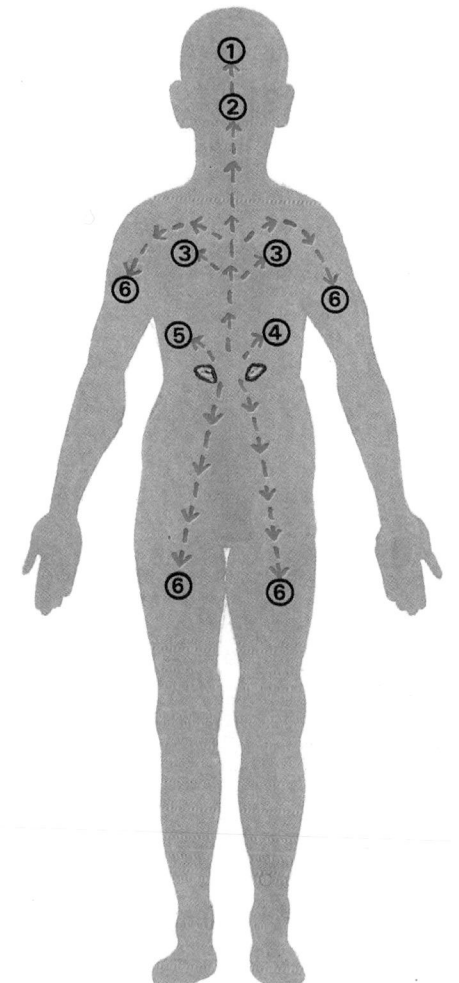

This is how adrenaline affects your body:

1 *Your pupils open to let in light.*
2 *Your flow of saliva stops.*
3 *You breathe faster to get more oxygen, and your heart pumps harder.*
4 *Your digestion stops.*
5 *Your liver sends extra food out to your muscles.*
6 *Your muscles are tense, ready for action.*

roamed around freely. But it still comes into use for modern "wild beasts" — playground bullies, cars, and so on. People can feel "threatened" by pleasant things too: taking a role in the school play, or tension before an important sports game starts.

As soon as the danger is over, another part of the automatic system switches on to calm you down. Adrenaline stops pouring out, breathing and heart rate slow down and useful work on such things as digestion and body-building starts up again.

It's adrenaline that makes you feel tense and excited during an **important game.**

What is anxiety?

Because nowadays much of the feeling of being threatened comes from inside yourself, and you can't do anything about it, all the energy that your fight or flight system has built up has nowhere to go. There is a risk that the pent-up energy will turn into anger — a nasty frustrated sort of tension. This is why some people have to teach themselves to relax and unwind. Otherwise, more and more adrenaline keeps pouring out, the system becomes overloaded and anxiety sets in.

Anxiety is a mild fear: "Will these people like me?" or "What will happen if I fail this test?" Anxiety is useful because it keys you up to do well. Everyone has some anxiety. Fear of the dark, of strangers, of moving to a new house or of not being popular, are all perfectly normal fears. Anxiety is only bad if it goes on for too long. If you are a slightly anxious person, you should learn to talk your fears away. Talking really does help — keeping quiet does not.

Right *As well as exercising your body, yoga teaches you how to relax your mind.*

17

Chapter 3

Health and Illness

Your brain and nervous system are also involved with your emotions — the way you feel. It is important to remember that different people have different temperaments. You cannot expect people to feel the same way you do.

Happiness and sadness

Some babies seem to be born happy, others seem to be afraid. But most babies are somewhere in between. They chuckle when they feel "good" — when they feel loved, interested, fed, warm and dry. They cry when they feel "bad" — when they feel unloved, bored, hungry, cold or wet.

The point to realize is that no one feels happy all the time. There are bound to be unhappy moments during each day. What is good is that unhappy feelings will pass — you will find yourself laughing again. Always remember this — unhappiness does go away.

Mental health is keeping a steady balance between feeling "good" and feeling "bad."

*A baby is happy when it feels warm, dry, well-fed
— and loved.*

What is mental disability?

Sad to say, a few babies are born with part of their brain damaged. There are different reasons why this happens; some reasons aren't known. There are also different types of brain damage. The most usual one is **cerebral palsy**. If the part of the brain that deals with movement is damaged, the baby will lose control of his arms and legs. If the part that deals with intelligence is damaged, the baby will be backward as he grows.

If you know someone who is disabled, you can help by being cheerful, pushing wheelchairs and offering to run errands for them. Never make fun of people who are disabled. They are likely to be far more sensitive than you.

Head injuries and concussion

In movies, you often see the hero getting knocked out in a fight. He crashes unconscious to the floor, comes round, and gets up to fight again. In real life, this doesn't happen. Any blow to the head which makes a person pass out (**concussion**) is always treated seriously. There is a risk that the brain has been damaged. The person must be taken to the hospital at once.

Below *In films, people jump up quickly after they've been knocked out, but that doesn't happen in real life.*

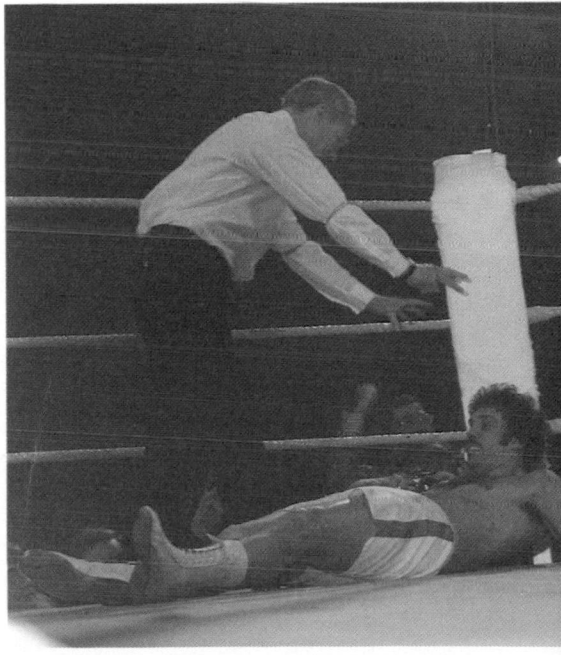

Left *Someone with brain damage may lose control over their muscles, but still be very intelligent.*

21

Infections

Meningitis is an infection of the meninges and, as you can guess, is very dangerous indeed.

Encephalitis is an infection of the brain itself. The person has terrible headaches, feels sleepy and may become unconscious. Again, this is very serious, especially if it happens to children or teenagers, and a doctor must be called. Luckily, both of these infections are quite rare.

What causes ordinary headaches?

Headaches come with all kinds of illnesses, but normally you shouldn't get them. If you are fit and healthy and get a headache, it is likely that you're not looking after yourself properly. Some of the things that can start a headache are too much noise, straining your eyes to read or watch TV, sitting in a stuffy room, not getting enough sleep or not drinking enough fluids. Work out what is going wrong, then change it.

However, if a headache is still there after a good night's sleep, go to your doctor. It's best not to take headache tablets. They only "mask" the pain and stop it for a while: they cannot make you well again by themselves.

Let in some fresh air if a stuffy room is giving you a headache.

Pain and anesthetics

If you fall down and hurt your knee, impulses are flashed to your brain and have to be interpreted there. It is your brain which changes the messages into the feeling of pain. The pain is registered in your brain, not in your knee. This is why a person who has a limb amputated (cut off) can still feel pain in the missing arm or leg. It is strange, but true; and it helps to remind you that you actually feel pain in your brain.

Have you ever had an **anesthetic?** Perhaps at the dentist's? An anesthetic is any drug used to deaden pain, or stop it from starting. A dentist uses a local anesthetic. It acts on one small area by deadening the receptor nerve endings.

If you go into the hospital for an operation, you will be given a general anesthetic.

The man on the far left is giving the patient general anesthetic.

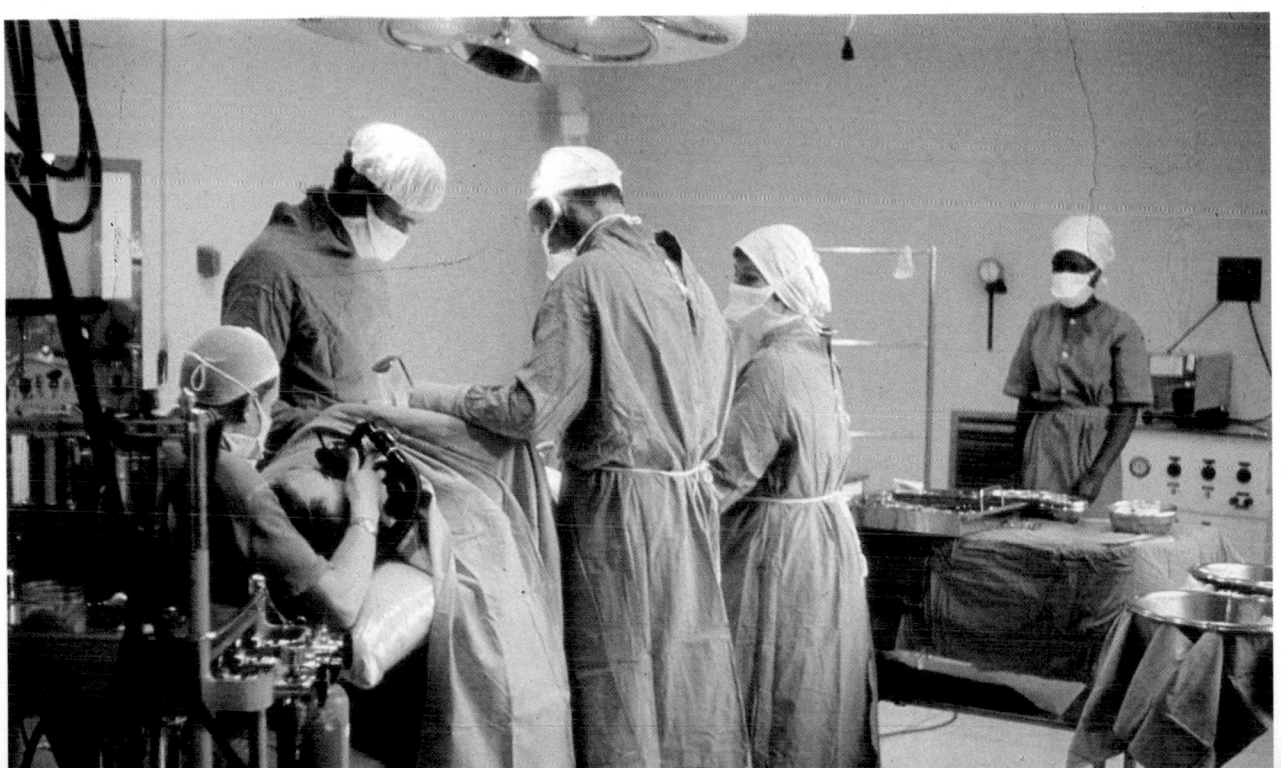

This does what its name suggests — it puts your brain and nervous system "to sleep" temporarily.

Anaesthetics make a few people feel peculiar as the effect wears off. Others may feel sick, but this doesn't last long. Imagine what it would be like if there were no anesthetics at all!

Sleep and dreams

Most growing children get plenty of sleep. The amount you need depends on your temperament. You will soon feel tired and drowsy if you don't have enough sleep. The growth hormone works best while you are asleep. So why not give it all the help you can?

Do you remember your dreams, or your nightmares? Have you ever walked or talked in your sleep? Some scientists think that dreams are for sorting out the new information which comes into your brain each day. As your unconscious mind goes over all the bits of new information, it comes up against a problem, or something it cannot understand. Your mind then tries to solve the mystery, working through one answer after another — which is why the dream keeps changing. Often you find the right answer, so "sleeping on it" actually can work sometimes.

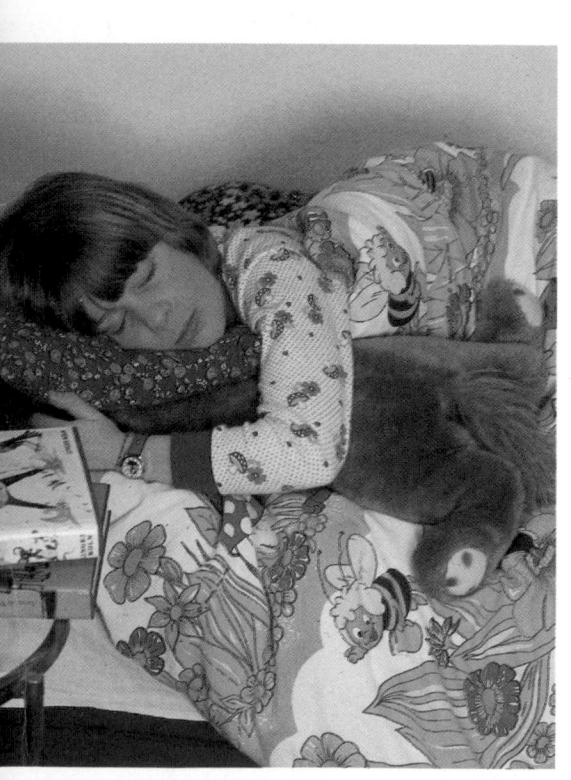

Do you sometimes dream about the book you were reading before you went to sleep?

Bad dreams and nightmares

Not all problems can be solved. There are times when a dream turns dark and frightening — a nightmare is a bad dream. It can be caused by anxiety: schoolwork not done, or an argument in the family. Try not to take these kinds of problems to bed. Finish your work, don't go to bed still angry with your family, and your dreams will not be frightening.

Remember, too, that dreams can be caused by simple things such as a cold in the head, going to bed overexcited, or eating too much just before bed. If you wake up from a bad dream, take a long drink of water, turn your thoughts to happy events, and you will soon drift peacefully back to sleep again.

Eating too much just before bed can give you nightmares.

Chapter 4

Your Hormone System

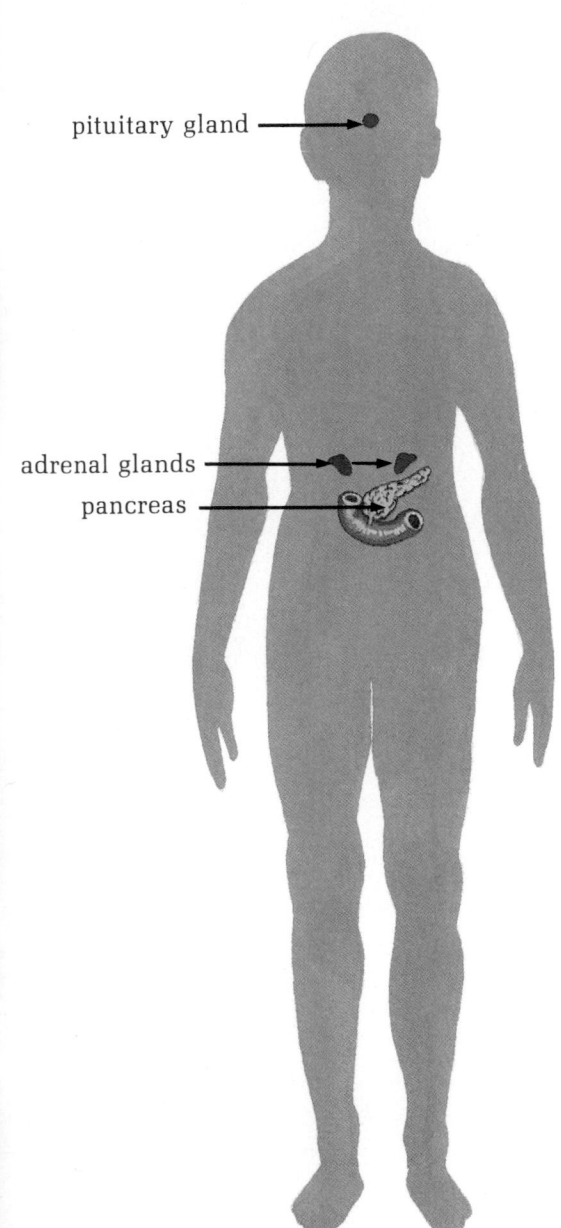

pituitary gland

adrenal glands

pancreas

What are hormones?

On page 15, you read how the hormone called adrenaline prepares you for flight or fight. There are other hormones which affect your body in different ways. Hormones are powerful chemicals made in special glands. You can see where the different glands are on the diagram.

These special glands are called the **endocrine system**. They have no tubes, and pour their hormones straight into the blood. Because hormones are so powerful, only small amounts are made. Hormones act together with your brain and nervous system to control the proper working of your body.

What do hormones control?

Each gland produces a different type of hormone. The **pituitary gland** is at the base of your brain. Although it is small (about the size of a cherry) it controls most of the other endocrine glands, and is often called the "master gland." One of the hormones the pituitary gland makes is the growth hormone. It is very important, especially in children. Too much of the growth hormone makes you too tall — this is called gigantism. Too little results in the opposite — dwarfism. Nowadays, these things don't happen because children's height and weight are regularly checked as they grow. Treatment is given if the growth hormone goes wrong. It is interesting to think that giants and dwarfs will soon only belong to fairy tales!

Around the front of your windpipe, just below your voice box, is a fairly large gland called the **thyroid**. This makes a hormone called **thyroxine**, which controls how quickly food and oxygen is "burned" in the cells of your body. If too little thyroxine is made during childhood the result is **cretinism** — stunted growth in body and mind. Too much thyroxine sets free too much energy — the person becomes restless, overactive and thin. Both of these conditions can be treated.

There are also four tiny glands called **parathyroids** buried inside the thyroid. They help to control the amount of **calcium** you have in your blood.

The **pancreas** makes the hormone **insulin**, which controls the amount of sugar in your body. A person who does not make enough insulin is called a diabetic. **Diabetes** is a serious condition but it can be treated with regular doses of insulin. In the diagram you can see there is a tube leading from the pancreas to the small intestine. This is because the pancreas also helps in digestion.

The two **adrenal glands** are on top of your

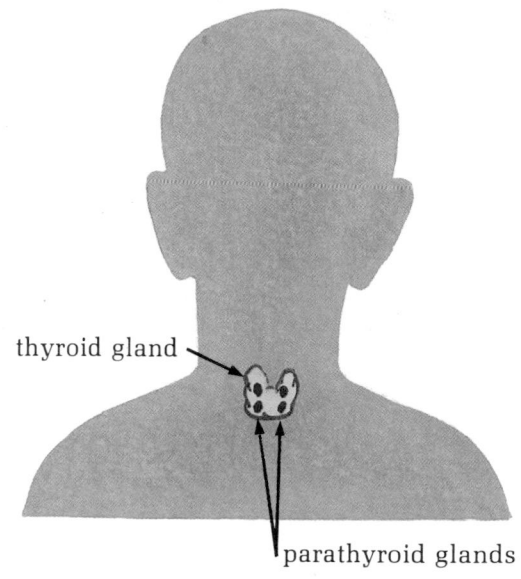

thyroid gland

parathyroid glands

kidneys. They make the hormone adrenaline, which has already been described in Chapter 2. Like the other endocrine glands, the adrenal glands make more than one hormone. The work of these other hormones is very varied and complex — such as reducing swellings and controlling the amount of fat stored in your body.

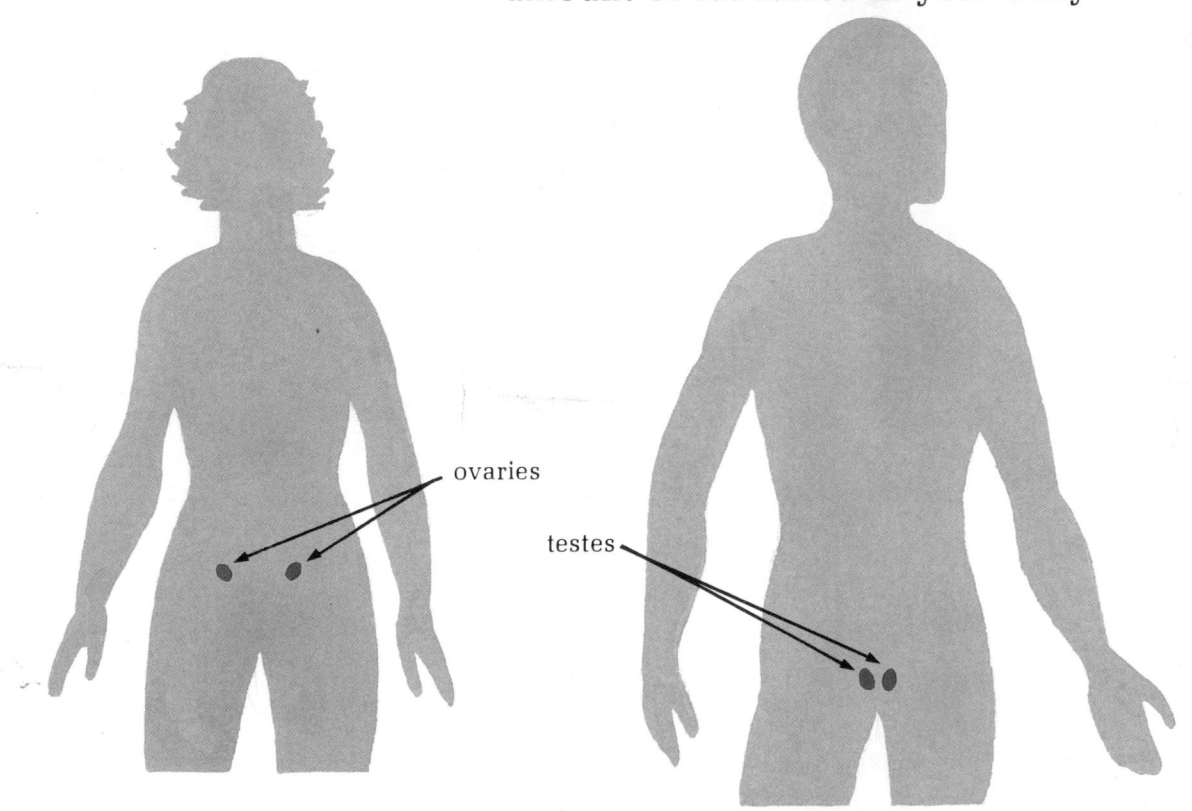

ovaries

testes

On these diagrams you can see the position of the male and female sex glands. The **ovaries** make the female sex hormones, **estrogen** and **progesterone**. The **testes** are the glands which make the male sex hormones. The most important one is called **testosterone**. These hormones control the changes in your body which happen as you grow from childhood to adulthood.

Caring for your nervous system

The things which do most harm to the delicate cells of your brain are alcohol and drugs. Stay clear of these. The thing that will do you most good is making sure you have regular rest and sleep. Remember, too, that your body and mind act together. If you are sick, you will feel miserable and anxious. And, the other way around, if you feel miserable and anxious you will be more likely to get sick.

Take care of your health, whether mental or physical, and your brain and nervous system will take care of you.

Whatever your age, plenty of rest and sleep is good for your nervous system.

Glossary

adrenaline The **hormone** made in the **adrenal glands** when you are frightened or excited. It prepares your body for action.

adrenal glands The two glands on top of your kidneys. They make **adrenaline** and other **hormones**.

anesthetic A drug that stops you from feeling pain. Local anesthetics make part of you numb; general anesthetic puts you to sleep.

autonomic system A part of your nervous system as the nerves controlling the rate of your heartbeat.

calcium A mineral your body needs to make strong bones and teeth.

capillaries The smallest blood tubes.

cerebellum The part of your brain that deals with your balance, and organizes your movements so that they are smoth and coordinated.

cerebral palsy A type of brain damage which a few babies are born with. The brain has no proper control over the arms and legs.

cerebrum The largest part of your brain. It controls your conscious actions, among other things.

concussion Becoming unconscious after a severe blow on the head.

cretinism If the **thyroid gland** does not make enough of the **hormone thyroxine** the person does not grow and is mentally backward.

diabetes An illness caused when the **pancreas** does not make enough **insulin**.

encephalitis A rare, but very dangerous infection of the brain.

endocrine system The system of glands that make **hormones**.

estrogen One of the female sex **hormones** made by the **ovaries**. You can read about the hormones in another book in this series — **How You Grow and Change**.

hormones Chemical messengers that help to control your health and growth.

insulin A **hormone** made in your **pancreas**. It controls the amount of sugar in your blood.

involuntary muscles The muscles

over which you have no control.

medulla The part of your brain at the top of your **spinal cord**. Among other things, it controls your breathing and heartbeat.

meninges The three linings that cover and protect your brain.

meningitis A dangerous infection of the **meninges**.

nerve fibers bundles of nerve tissue which carry messages to and from your brain.

nerve impulses The waves of electrical and chemical change that travels along **nerve fibers**.

overies The two female glands which make the hormones **estrogen** and **progesterone**.

pancreas The gland near your liver that makes **insulin**.

parathyroids Four small glands inside the **thyroid gland**. Among other things, the control the amount of **calcium** in your blood.

pituitary gland The gland at the base of your skull that makes the growth **hormone**, and controls the other **endocrine glands**.

progesterone One of the female sex **hormones** made in the **ovaries**.

proteins The "building blocks" of your cells. They are found in foods such as meat, fish, eggs and milk.

reflex action An automatic action you are born with and cannot

control, such as the knee jerk reflex.

saliva The fluid which keeps your mouth moist, and aids digestion.

semicircular canals Three tiny canals inside your ear which send information to your brain to control your balance. You can read more about them in another book in this series — **Your Senses**.

spinal cord The thick bundle of nerve tissue which leads down from your brain, inside your spine.

stretch receptors Nerve endings which collect information about what is going on inside you. You can read about receptors in another book in this series — **Your Senses**.

stroke Brain damage which happens when something goes wrong with the brain's blood supply.

testes The two male glands which make the sex **hormone** called **testosterone**. You can find out more about this hormone in another book in this series — **How You Grow and Change**.

testosterone The male sex **hormone** which is made in the **testes**.

thyroid gland The gland in your neck which makes **thyroxine**.

thyroxine A **hormone** made by the **thyroid gland**. It controls the rate at which your body burns energy.

Index

Picture acknowledgements Cover: Jerry Mason/Science Photo Library; BBC 23; Sally and Richard Greenhill 13, 14, 19, 25, 29; Alan Hutchison Library 9 (Hilary Andrews), 22; Don Morley 21; Rex Features Ltd 8; John Watney Photo Library 5; Wayland Picture Library 10, 12, 16; Zefa 17, 20, 24.